Baptism

A Bible Study Wordbook for Kids

by Richard E. Todd

This Wordbook Belongs To . . .

WingSpread Publishers

Chicago, Illinois

Message to Parents/ Teachers

In order for this Bible study wordbook to be profitable for your children, your help is needed. Try to be available to answer questions that might arise, but please, as much as possible, allow your children to discover these important Bible truths for themselves.

Instructions For Parents/Teachers

1. This Bible study wordbook entitled *Baptism* has been written to help you determine if your student has invited Jesus into his/her heart and is ready to be baptized. The *Baptism* wordbook is part of a series that is most beneficial when used in combination with the others. Other wordbooks in this series include *Salvation, Church, Giving* and *Communion.*

2. Allow your student to study the material on his/her own as much as possible. Children in early elementary grades might need assistance in completing some sections of the wordbook.

3. The student is asked if he/she has received Jesus. Check his/her response in chapter 2. Any response should be a beginning for discussion.

4. Chapter 3 discusses the method of baptism. A student's understanding about the method of baptism can be increased by watching someone else be baptized before he/she is baptized.

5. Grade the fill-in sections and the final quiz. Review the answers and be sure your student understands the issues involved. The quiz answers are listed on page 3.

6. Your student should understand why he/she wants to be baptized. If he/she does not, then it would be wise to wait. The experience of obedience by baptism must be to the Lord and not because relatives have been baptized or the student has been told he/she should do this (then he/she is only pleasing people). Talk to your pastor about your church's guidelines for baptism.

7. Remembering the special time of receiving Jesus as Savior and Lord is a most important thing for children. It might prove quite valuable to interview your child and make an audio or video recording of it. Ask them to share the circumstances of their salvation. You can prepare them prior to starting the interview, but once you start you should avoid any temptation to prompt. A minute or two of recorded conversation at a young age may be all that is needed to reinforce their decision later in life. Here are some questions you might ask during the interview:

- *Is Jesus in your life?*
- *How did it happen?*
- *How do you know Jesus is in your life?*
- *Who was there?*
- *When did it happen?*
- *Why do you want to be baptized?*
- *Where will it happen?*
- *What does it mean to be baptized?*

8. The student is asked to write the names of two people they would like to invite the day they are baptized. Your assistance may be needed to place a phone call to someone or help your student to write a letter of invitation.

9. The student is asked in chapter 4 if he/she has ever seen someone be baptized. If he/she has not, you might want to arrange for him/her to see a baptism before he/she is baptized.

10. The illustration of the Trinity communicated in baptism should not be overlooked but rather emphasized.

11. Most churches prepare a baptism certificate and give it to the person who was baptized. Make sure this is done and that the student takes it home to keep as a reminder of this special event in his/her Christian life.

QUIZ ANSWERS (PAGES 20–21):
MULTIPLE CHOICE: 1. d **2.** b **3.** d **4.** b **RIGHT WAY, WRONG WAY:**
Right-hand picture **TRUE/FALSE: 1.** T **2.** T **3.** T **4.** T **5.** T

Pastor Richard E. Todd is Senior Pastor of Community Grace Brethren Church in Whittier, California. He first joined the staff there in 1982 as Associate Pastor and became Senior Pastor in 1987. He and his wife, Claudia, have three sons: Ryan, Riley, and Rory.

BaPtiSM

WingSpread Publishers
Chicago, Illinois

www.moodypublishers.com

An imprint of Moody Publishers

Baptism: A Bible Study Wordbook for Kids
by Richard E. Todd
ISBN: 978-1-60066-194-5
Printed by Versa Press in East Peoria, IL – 4/21

10

Cover illustrations by Rick Hemphill
Interior design by Pam Fogle
Various inside illustrations by
Alma Escalera Miller and Ron Kellner

Originally published by Crosswalk Resources

Scripture taken from the
INTERNATIONAL CHILDREN'S BIBLE®,
©1986, 1988, 1999 by Thomas Nelson, Inc.
Used by permission.

WHY DO PEOPLE GET BAPTIZED?

PEOPLE GET BAPTIZED TO TELL OTHERS THEY HAVE JOINED GOD'S FAMILY.

"Then those people who accepted what Peter said [about Jesus] were baptized." Acts 2:41

Paul explained to them about believing in Jesus. Then "they were baptized in the name of the Lord Jesus." Acts 19:5

Most of us can remember at least one special Christmas when we received a certain gift we had hoped so much for. It was exciting to open that one gift of love. We could hardly wait to tell others about what we had received.

What is one special gift that you received for your last birthday or Christmas? Perhaps someone in your family or a friend gave it to you.

MY SPECIAL GIFT WAS _____

_____

_____

Just like opening that special gift you received at Christmas, there is excitement when Christ comes into our lives bringing His special gift of eternal life. It is so special that we will want to tell others about it.

 "God gives us the free gift of life forever in Christ Jesus our Lord." Romans 6:23

Baptism is a special way of showing your neighbors and friends that Jesus is in your life and you are a member of His family.

 **PeopLe Get BaptizeD to SHow tHeY aRe DoiNG WHat JesUs waNts tHeM to Do.**

 Jesus said, "So go and make followers of all people in the world. Baptize them in the name of the Father and the Son and the Holy Spirit. Teach them to obey everything that I have told you." Matthew 28:19–20

 Jesus also said, "You are my friends if you do what I command you." John 15:14

WHY SHoULD We oBeY JesUs?

Baptism is one special way of obeying Jesus. There are other ways you can obey Him.

STUDY THE PICTURES BELOW AND _CIRCLE_ THE PICTURES THAT SHOW PEOPLE OBEYING JESUS.

WHO CAN BE BAPTIZED?

PEOPLE WHO HAVE JOINED GOD'S FAMILY CAN BE BAPTIZED.

The Bible says, "An angel of the Lord spoke to **Philip**. The angel said, 'Get ready and go **south**. Go to the road that leads down to Gaza from Jerusalem—the desert road.' So Philip got ready and went. On the road he saw a man from Ethiopia. He was an important officer in the service of **Candace**, the queen of the Ethiopians. He was responsible for taking care of all her money. He had gone to Jerusalem to **worship**, and now he was on his way home. He was sitting in his **chariot** and reading from the book of **Isaiah**, the **prophet**.

"Philip asked, 'Do you understand what you are reading?' He answered, 'How can I understand? I need someone to explain it to me!' Then he invited Philip to climb in and sit with him. Philip began to speak. He started with this same Scripture and told the man the Good News about Jesus.

"While they were traveling down the road, they came to some water. The officer said, 'Look! Here is water! What is stopping me from being baptized?' Philip answered, 'If you **believe** with all your heart, you can.' The officer said, 'I believe that Jesus Christ is the Son of God.' Then the officer commanded the chariot to stop. Both Philip and the officer went down into the water, and Philip **baptized** him." Acts 8:26–28, 30–31, 35–38

WHAT HAPPENED FIRST?

Write the number 1 in the circle beside the event that happened first. Next, write a number 2 in the circle beside the event that happened second. Now write in the third and fourth events.

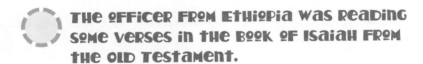 THE OFFICER FROM ETHIOPIA WAS READING SOME VERSES IN THE BOOK OF ISAIAH FROM THE OLD TESTAMENT.

 PHILIP BAPTIZED THE MAN FROM ETHIOPIA.

THE OFFICER COMMANDED THE CHARIOT TO STOP.

 THE OFFICER FROM ETHIOPIA BELIEVED THAT JESUS CHRIST IS THE SON OF GOD.

CROSSWORD PUZZLE

ACROSS

1 Who was the boss of the officer from Ethiopia?

3 What Philip did to the officer.

6 The book of the Bible that the officer was reading from.

8 The direction Philip went on the road.

9 The title of Isaiah (his job) mentioned in these verses.

DOWN

2 What the officer was sitting in.

4 What Philip told the officer he must do before he could be baptized.

5 Name of the man who baptized the Ethiopian officer.

7 The Ethiopian officer went to Jerusalem to_____.

Look back at the story on pages 8 and 9 to find the right words to this crossword puzzle.

HINT: *Look at the words that are underlined.*

The followers of Jesus were baptized after they joined God's family.

When you invite Jesus into your life, you are joining God's family. **Once you are a member of God's family, you can be baptized.**

 "Some people did accept him [Jesus]. They believed in him. To them he gave the right to become children of God." John 1:12

 "Can anyone keep these people from being baptized with water? They have received the Holy Spirit just as we did!" Acts 10:47

Have you joined God's family and invited Jesus into your life?

 YES, I HAVE ALREADY JOINED GOD'S FAMILY. *Fill out the Certificate of Spiritual Birth on page 25 as a special reminder of your decision.*

 NO, I HAVE NOT JOINED GOD'S FAMILY.

WOULD YOU LIKE TO JOIN GOD'S FAMILY NOW? _____

IF NOT, PLEASE EXPLAIN WHY YOU WOULD NOT LIKE TO.

_____

_____

_____

How is a Person Baptized?

A person is baptized in water.

"Philip and the officer went down into the water, and Philip baptized him." Acts 8:38

The word *baptize* means "to put in the water." And that's just what Philip did to the man from the country of Ethiopia . . . he put him in the water and baptized him. When you are baptized, you will be in the water.

People are baptized in many different places. Philip used a river. A church often uses something that looks a little like a swimming pool.

CHECK THE CIRCLE THAT DESCRIBES THE FOLLOWING PICTURE:

RIGHT WAY

WRONG WAY

WORD SEARCH

Baptism is a special way of showing others that Jesus is in your life and you are a member of His family. Can you find the baptism words listed below in the word search?

BAPTIZING   NATIONS   SPIRIT
COMMANDED   OBEY   TESTIMONY
DISCIPLES   PHILIP   WATER
FATHER   SON

```
G Z A R D N I H A T V W S L S
E U R Z V Z A Q R I C E U P G
X Q D N H N E T G I L X I Q E
O E E B M M M H I P K R W Y J
D D D W R R L W I O I D T T M
A E N O H C E C N T N Y V J A
N H A X Z G S T G I H S V C F
Z U M C K I N E A K Y S X N A
Y U M X D I J I D W O O D R T
E N O A D X P Y Z F L V C O H
B D C Q X T E S T I M O N Y E
O O P I L I H P G P T O Q Y R
P B W M L K K K G G S P D P X
C K O A D M A Q T B Q Q A D D
W B V K F T W A L E O K G B A
```

Puzzle created by *Puzzlemaker* from Discovery Channel School. Used by permission.

COLORING PAGE

You can invite Jesus into your life and join God's family right now by praying like this:

DEAR JESUS,
THANK YOU FOR LOVING ME ENOUGH TO
DIE ON THE CROSS TO PAY FOR MY SIN. I
KNOW I DO WRONG THINGS. PLEASE
FORGIVE ME FOR ALL THE WRONG THINGS
THAT I'VE DONE. I WANT YOU TO
COME INTO MY LIFE. HELP ME
TO CHOOSE TO DO WHAT YOU
WANT ME TO DO. THANK
YOU FOR MAKING ME YOUR
CHILD AND A MEMBER OF
YOUR FAMILY.
AMEN.

You should wait to be baptized until you have joined God's family. You should wait because when you are baptized you are saying **(on the outside)** that Jesus is in your heart and life **(on the inside)**.

Once you have joined God's family by inviting Jesus into your life, fill out the certificate on page 25.

You can learn more about joining God's family in the *Salvation* wordbook.

A PERSON IS BAPTIZED BY SOMEONE ELSE.

 "I [the Apostle Paul] . . . baptized the family of Stephanas." 1 Corinthians 1:16

 "Philip baptized him [the officer from Ethiopia]." Acts 8:38

You can't baptize yourself, and machines don't baptize people. Philip baptized the man from Ethiopia and you will probably be baptized by someone at your church. Usually your pastor or another church leader will baptize you.

CHECK THE CIRCLE THAT DESCRIBES EACH OF THE FOLLOWING PICTURES:

RIGHT WAY   **WRONG WAY**

RIGHT WAY   **WRONG WAY**

A PERSON IS BAPTIZED WHILE OTHER PEOPLE ARE WATCHING.

 "Then those people who accepted what Peter said [about Jesus] were baptized. About 3,000 people . . ."
Acts 2:41

Because you are telling people that Jesus is in your life when you are baptized, there will be people watching and listening.

WRITE THE NAMES OF TWO PEOPLE YOU WOULD LIKE TO INVITE TO COME AND WATCH YOU BE BAPTIZED:

PERSON 1 _____

PERSON 2 _____

CHECK THE CIRCLE THAT DESCRIBES THE FOLLOWING PICTURE:

 RIGHT WAY

WRONG WAY

A PERSON IS BAPTIZED IN THE NAME OF THE FATHER, THE SON (THAT'S JESUS) AND THE HOLY SPIRIT.

"Go and make followers of all people in the world. Baptize them in the name of the Father and the Son and the Holy Spirit." Matthew 28:19

You will be baptized in special honor of the Father, the Son and the Holy Spirit for the part each has played in your salvation.

CHECK THE CIRCLE THAT DESCRIBES EACH OF THE FOLLOWING PICTURES:

WHAT HaVe YOU LeaRNeD aBOUT BaPTiSM?

MULTiPLe CHOiCe

Answer the questions as best you can without help from anyone else. **You may look back in the wordbook for answers.**

1. BeiNG BaPTiZeD iS _____ *(Write the letter of the correct answer on each line.)*

    a. something all children do.

    b. only for children whose parents go to church.

    c. for children who like hamburgers.

    d. for anyone who has Jesus in his/her life.

2. BaPTiSM MeaNS _____

    a. like when my Sunday school teacher is speaking.

    b. a special event when someone is put under water.

    c. to pray for a friend.

3. JeSUS SaiD THaT a PeRSON SHOULD Be BaPTiZeD _____

    a. to be saved.

    b. to get lots of money.

    c. to go to heaven.

    d. to show others that Jesus is in his or her life.

4. JeSUS WiLL COMe iNTO a PeRSON'S LiFe _____

    a. when a person goes to church.

    b. when a person asks Jesus to come into his/her life.

    c. when the person reads the Bible.

RIGHT WAY, WRONG WAY

Circle the picture that shows the way the Bible teaches us to be baptized.

TRUE/FALSE

Write **T** for true or **F** for false in the space provided.

_____ **1.** People are baptized in the name of the Father, the Son and the Holy Spirit.

_____ **2.** One reason people get baptized is to show that their sins have been washed away.

_____ **3.** Jesus said being baptized is important.

_____ **4.** The Bible teaches that a person should be baptized to show others that Jesus is in his or her life.

_____ **5.** People are baptized with water.

NOW HAVE A PARENT OR TEACHER GRADE YOUR QUIZ.

YOUR TESTIMONY

On the day of your baptismal service, there may be an opportunity for you to give a short testimony of how you came to Christ.

A testimony is telling others what Christ has done for you. It doesn't have to be long; just tell where, when, how and who prayed with you when you asked Jesus into your life. You can also tell what difference Jesus has made in your life and why you want to be baptized.

Write out your testimony below. Remember, the most important thing to tell is when you asked Jesus into your life.

ARE YOU READY TO BE BAPTIZED?

PLACE A CHECK ON EACH LINE ACCORDING TO THE INSTRUCTIONS.

○ **PLACE A CHECK HERE IF YOU HAVE INVITED JESUS TO COME INTO YOUR LIFE.**

○ **PLACE A CHECK HERE IF YOU HAVE EVER WATCHED A BAPTISM AT YOUR CHURCH.** *If you have not seen a baptism at your church, ask your parent or teacher if you can do so before you are baptized.*

○ **PLACE A CHECK IF YOU TOOK THE QUIZ ON PAGES 20–21 AND HAD YOUR PARENT OR TEACHER GRADE IT.**

○ **PLACE A CHECK HERE IF YOU WANT TO GET BAPTIZED.**

(CONTINUED ON NEXT PAGE)

PLACE A CHECK HERE IF YOUR PARENT(S) SAYS IT IS OKAY FOR YOU TO BE BAPTIZED.

 HAVE YOU WRITTEN OUT YOUR TESTIMONY? IF SO, PLACE A CHECK HERE.

 DID YOU WRITE THE NAMES OF TWO PEOPLE ON PAGE 18 WHOM YOU WOULD LIKE TO INVITE TO COME TO YOUR BAPTISM? *If not, turn back and try to do it now. Then place a check in this space even if you couldn't think of two people to invite.*

If you were able to place a check on each line according to the instructions, then you are ready to be baptized. Talk to your pastor or have your parents talk to your pastor about setting a date for your baptism.

FILL IN THE CERTIFICATE ON THE NEXT PAGE YOURSELF.

Tell two people who are very special to you about the time you joined God's family and invited Jesus into your heart. Then ask them to sign your certificate. They will be your witnesses because they listened to what you said.

Certificate
of
Spiritual Birth

I, _____
(your name)

was born into God's family

on _____
(date)

at _____
(place)

_____.

witnesses:

1. _____

2. _____